AMAZING WONDERS

CHICHÉN ITZÁ

BY LORI DITTMER

CREATIVE EDUCATION • CREATIVE PAPERBACKS

Published by Creative Education and Creative Paperbacks
P.O. Box 227, Mankato, Minnesota 56002
Creative Education and Creative Paperbacks
are imprints of The Creative Company
www.thecreativecompany.us

Design by The Design Lab
Art direction by Graham Morgan
Edited by Jill Kalz

Images by Getty (Erich Andres/United Archives, Geography Photos), iStock (pop_jop), Pexels (Israel Albornoz, Israyosoy S), Unsplash (Alex Azabache, Andy McCune, Chad Peltola, Cody McLain, Filip Gielda, Julie Sd, Luis Aceves, Marv Watson, Matt Hanns Schroeter), Wikimedia Commons (Frederick Catherwood)

Library of Congress Cataloging-in-Publication Data
Names: Dittmer, Lori, author.
Title: Chichén Itzá / by Lori Dittmer.
Description: Mankato, Minnesota : Creative Education and Creative Paperbacks, [2025] | Series: Amazing wonders | Includes bibliographical references and index. | Audience: Ages 6–9 | Audience: Grades 2–3 | Summary: "An elementary-level introduction to the ancient Mexican city of Chichén Itzá, covering how, when, and why the Maya built the famous wonder. Includes captions, on-page definitions, additional resources, and an index"—Provided by publisher.
Identifiers: LCCN 2023042462 (print) | LCCN 2023042463 (ebook) | ISBN 9781640268562 (library binding) | ISBN 9781682774069 (paperback) | ISBN 9798889890188 (ebook)
Subjects: LCSH: Chichén Itzá Site (Mexico)—Juvenile literature. | Mayas—Mexico—Yucatán (State)—Juvenile literature. | Yucatán (Mexico : State)—Juvenile literature.
Classification: LCC F1435.1.C5 D58 2025 (print) | LCC F1435.1.C5 (ebook) | DDC 972/.6—dc23/eng/20231002
LC record available at https://lccn.loc.gov/2023042462
LC ebook record available at https://lccn.loc.gov/2023042463

Printed in China

Table of Contents

Chichén Itzá is a famous ancient city in Mexico. Its name means "the mouth of the water witch's well." It may also mean "by the well of the Itzá people." Thousands of people once lived there.

Stone posts outside the Temple of the Warriors once held up a giant roof.

People threw gold and other riches into the Sacred Cenote as offerings to their water god.

Chichén Itzá is on the Yucatán Peninsula. Its **ruins** are surrounded by jungle. Many natural wells, called cenotes (seh-NOH-tayz), lie nearby. The wells formed easily in the soft limestone rock. They supplied water for the city's people.

ruins structures that have become damaged and broken down over time

The Maya carved stone snakes to honor the great god Kukulcan.

The Maya people built Chichén Itzá during the sixth century. It was a center for buying and selling goods. Later, the Toltec people invaded the city. They added their own buildings and **monuments**.

monuments structures built to remember people or events

The main temple is a stepped pyramid made of gray limestone.

To build the city, the Maya first made the ground flat. Then they brought in limestone blocks. They may have used ramps or pulleys to move them. Sidewalks were laid to connect many of the buildings.

pulleys simple machines used to move or lift heavy objects

The observatory is called El Caracol ("The Snail") because of the spiral staircase inside.

The Maya were experts at math. They studied the stars and watched the sun move across the sky. They built an **observatory** in Chichén Itzá. Its narrow windows were made to frame certain stars and the planet Venus.

observatory a place from which to view events in the sky

The Maya played a ball game like soccer. Players tried to send a ball through rings without using their hands. Chichén Itzá has a playing area for this sport. It is the largest area of its kind in North or South America.

The wall at each end of the playing area has a stone ring or goal.

The people of Chichén Itzá worshipped a god named Kukulcan. They built a temple for him in the shape of a pyramid. The temple may have been used as a calendar. The position of the sun would signal when to plant crops.

Kukulcan's temple has 365 steps, one for each day of the year.

Chichén Itzá was mostly forgotten until its rediscovery in the mid-1800s.

Spanish explorers arrived in Chichén Itzá during the 1500s. By then, most people had moved away. We do not know why they left. A drought may have caused them to look for better land to grow crops.

drought a long period with no rain or low levels of rain

People continue to study Chichén Itzá. The city reminds us that people used math and science to create structures long before modern technology. It is an amazing wonder!

Roughly two million people visit the main temple in Chichén Itzá each year.

Wonder Spotlight: Shadow Snakes

El Castillo

("The Castle") is the main temple in Chichén Itzá. At the top is a carving of the god Kukulcan. At the base of one staircase are two snake heads carved in stone. Each spring and fall, the setting sun casts a special shadow. It looks like a snake sliding down the steps. The shadowy body connects to one of the stone heads at the bottom.

Read More

Green, Sara. *Chichén Itzá.* Minneapolis: Bellwether Media, 2021.

Spanier, Kristine. *Chichén Itzá.* Minneapolis: Jump!, 2022.

Van, R. L. *Mexico.* Minneapolis: Big Buddy Books, 2023.

Websites

Britannica Kids: Chichén Itzá
https://kids.britannica.com/kids/article/Chichén-Itzá/474431
Learn the basics about this wonder.

DK Findout!: Chichén Itzá
https://www.dkfindout.com/us/earth/landmarks-world/chichen-itza
This site includes a labeled picture of El Castillo.

Note: Every effort has been made to ensure that the websites listed above are suitable for children, that they have educational value, and that they contain no inappropriate material. However, because of the nature of the Internet, it is impossible to guarantee that these sites will remain active indefinitely or that their contents will not be altered.

Index